T0197373

Matthew
And The
Magical
Star

To order additional copies of this book, contact:
Xlibris
1-888-795-4274
www.Xlibris.com
Orders@Xlibris.com

Dedicated to my

Grandson, Matthew Anduha

And all my Grandchildren

But especially to

The Faith and the Drive

behind my creativity

my Wife

Claire

Heaven is a very busy place, with people leaving life on Earth and coming to be with their family and friends, and with the new ones leaving Heaven to be born and start a new life on Earth. Those who came from Earth were to study to be angels, some to care for the new ones until their time to be born and some to help those they've left behind on Earth.

Now, Matthew was a new one who had waited a long, long time to be born. It always seemed that when it was his turn to be born that he was overlooked. But he tried to be patient, because he knew that when he was to be born he would be very special. Matthew and his friend Adam would busy themselves by roaming through the clouds and making them angry so that they would grumble and flash their lightening eyes at them.

But what they liked most was listening to St. Peter talk of all the people he had met and how wonderful it was on Earth.

3

Now, on the day that they were to announce who would be the new ones to be born, everyone rushed to the Great Hall. When the Archangel appeared, all were hushed. Matthew waited patiently as the names were read; " Ashley, Denzyl, Evan, Hailey, Jayden, Liam" and so on and so on until they reached the 'M's. "Marc, Mary, Marie, Matthew, Na Na, Ronald, Walker".

When Matthew finally realizes that his name has been called he and Adam fly off in joy. They zoomed down the streets of heaven, around the pearly gates and soared like rockets through the clouds.

Matthew and Adam rushed back to see the list that the Archangel had posted to see when he was to be born. There on the list, at last, was his name and the date he was to be born: "Matthew..... Earth date; December 25th".

The next day, Matthew had to meet with the Archangel to find out all about his family on Earth. But, as he entered the Great Hall, everything was hushed. Everyone was whispering and scurrying around. The Archangel had just come out from speaking with God and had a very serious look on his face. He went up to the list of those who were to be born and scratched off all the names for Earth Date December 25th. Matthew was shattered and wanted to ask the Archangel why this had happened, but he was afraid to approach him.

Matthew went to St. Peter to see if he knew why the names had been crossed off. St. Peter said, "God has a great announcement to make to all here in Heaven. You will hear why then."

8

That afternoon, when the trumpets sounded the approach of God, all rushed to the Great Hall. All but Matthew. As all gathered to hear the word of God, Matthew stayed back, not wanting to listen or show how hurt he was. God Said; "My people on Earth have forgotten to honor me and keep my commandments. They care more for their little material things than for their God. They need to be reminded that I am the one true God. That I alone give them the food they eat, the water they drink and the air they breathe. I will send my son to be born on Earth and walk among them to remind them of me and my gifts. On December 25th, my son will be born to a woman called Mary, beloved of Joseph."

Matthew was very hurt and flew off to hide in the clouds, where no one could see him cry. Adam looked all over for his friend but couldn't find him anywhere.

Then God reached down and picked up Matthew. And God said, "How could you think that I did not have great plans for you? I have kept you here in Heaven to help with the arrival of my son on Earth. Come with me and we will make our plans."

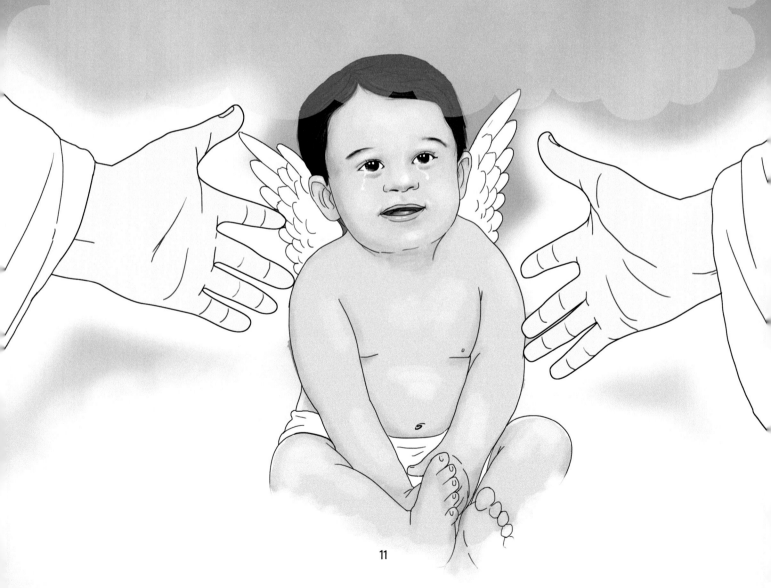

11

God took Matthew, Adam, St. Peter and the Archangel into his chambers and began to speak of the day when his Son would be born. "We must be sure that the just and the humble know of his birth and come to pay him homage. Thinking of all the beautiful lights now within infinity Matthew thought that one great star should shine down on Earth and the place where God's Son was to be born. "We will have the Angels tell only the good and the wise of your son's arrival and they can follow the light." Matthew said. With that God said, "This is the task that I have saved you for. You shall carry the light into infinity to shine down on my Son. This honor I bestow upon you."

When it neared the time for the birth of God's Son on earth, everyone was busy and running about. The angels of Heaven were sent to Earth to seek out three wise men and three just kings to go and witness the coming of the savior. God called Matthew to the great hall and gave him a beautiful golden vase. "This is the light that shall fill the Heavens to announce the coming of my Son to Man. This great light will guide the wise and the just to him. You must carry it to the very edge of infinity and release it to shine down upon the place where my Son is.

13

Matthew took the golden vase and flew off to infinity. Higher and higher he flew, to the very edge of infinity itself. There he opened the vase and took out the light. He held it high and with great pride exclaimed; "This day the son of God is born. He shall be the light of the world."

14

Then an angel of the Lord stood before some shepherds on earth, and the glory of the Lord shone around her. "Do not be afraid, for behold, I bring you good tidings of great joy which will be to all people. For there is born to you this day in the city of David, a savior, who is Christ the Lord. And this will be the sign to you: you will find a babe wrapped in swaddling clothes, lying in a manger." And suddenly there was with the angel a multitude of the Heavenly host, praising God and saying;

"Glory to God in the Highest,

And on Earth Peace,

Good will toward men!"

Printed in the United States
By Bookmasters